Contents

Any words appearing in the text in bold,
like this, are explained in the Glossary.

What are ramps and wedges?

ramp

A machine is a man-made **device**. All machines help us to do jobs. Ramps and wedges are very useful machines. A ramp is a long slope, like this sloping plank.

narrow end

A wedge is like two slopes joined together. Here is a wedge made of wood. You can see a slope down toward the narrow end, and a slope underneath that it's resting on.

What do ramps and wedges do?

We use **pushes** and **pulls** to lift and move things. A ramp makes it easier to move things up or downwards. This ramp makes it easier to load a truck.

A wedge is a machine that pushes things apart. Pushing on the end of a wedge makes the wedge's sides push outwards. These wedges are helping to split a piece of wood.

How does a ramp work?

A ramp makes it easier to move an object upwards. A big effort is needed to empty a bucket of rubble by lifting it straight up from the ground.

Now the workman has put a ramp up to the top of the skip. He has moved the bucket upwards by walking up the ramp. This was much easier than lifting it.

Simple ramps

These ramps are on the back of a rescue truck. The car is **pulled** up the ramps on to the truck. It would be very difficult to lift the car on to the truck.

This is a wheelchair ramp. It makes it easy for the person in the chair to get on to the bus. Going up a step in a wheelchair would be very tricky.

Path and road ramps

Roads are often ramps, too. A gently sloping road is easier for a car to drive along than a steep road. Motorways have gentle slopes. This helps to keep cars moving fast.

To get the boat out of the river, these rafters use a ramp. They tie the boat on to a **winch** with a rope. Then they **pull** the boat up the ramp.

Different ramp shapes

Some ramps are built in strange shapes. This zig-zag road has many ramps, going one way then the other. It is easier to drive up the zig-zag road than straight up the hill.

This ramp goes round in circles as it goes up from one floor to the next in a car park. A round ramp takes up less space than lots of straight ramps.

How does a wedge work?

The shape of a wedge changes the direction of a push. Pushing on the flat end of the wedge makes the sides **push** outwards. You can see the wedge shape of this axe.

The axe is splitting the log. The woodcutter hammers downwards. The wedge-shaped axe head pushes outwards. The wedge shape also makes the push bigger. This makes it easy to split the wood.

Simple wedges

blade

Here are some simple wedges doing jobs. The **blade** on this snow plough is a wedge. As the plough **pushes** the blade forwards, the blade pushes the snow to the side.

This worker is using a wedge to split the rock. A small push on the wedge makes a big push on the rock, splitting it apart.

Wedges for cutting

Tools that cut have **blades**. The sharp edge of the blade is a wedge. This tool is called a **chisel**. The wedge-shaped blade cuts into the wood.

Your front teeth are like wedge-shaped cutting tools. When you bite into an apple, your front teeth slice through the flesh, splitting off chunks of it.

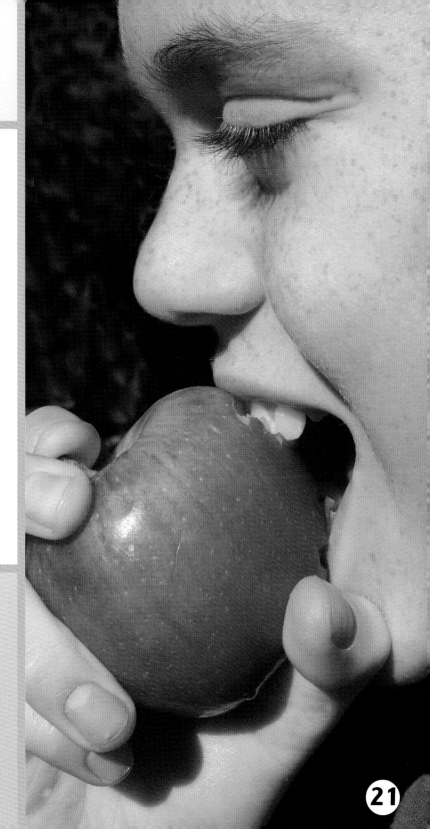

Wedges for piercing

Things like nails and pins have sharp points on the end. A sharp point works like a wedge. The point on this sewing needle **pushes** the layers of cloth apart as it pierces downwards.

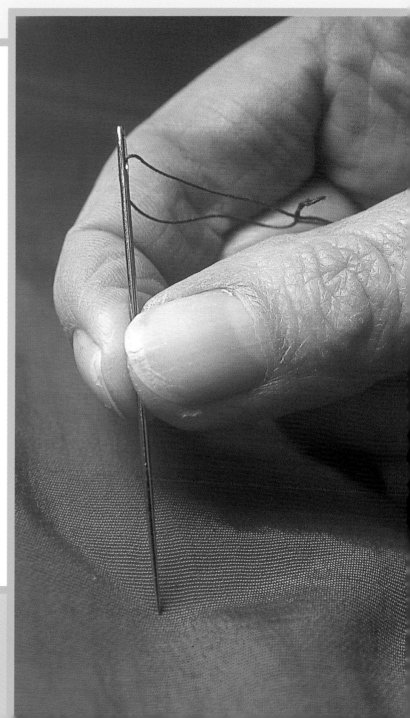

There is a sharp **chisel** on the end of this **pneumatic** road drill. The drill hammers to chisel down into the road. This works as a wedge and splits the hard road surface apart.

Wedges for holding

chock

chock

Wedges are useful for jamming into gaps.
A jammed wedge can hold things in place.
Here special wedges called chocks stop the
plane from rolling forward.

If you try to shut this door, the rubber wedge **pushes** up on the door and down on the floor. This stops the wedge sliding, so the wedge keeps the door open.

Ramps and wedges in machines

Many big machines have ramps and wedges in them, like the **bow** of a ship. Its wedge shape **pushes** the ice and water aside, making it easy for the ship to move forwards.

plough blade

A **plough** has many metal blades. Each one has a wedge that splits up the **soil** as the tractor pulls the plough. The blade also turns the soil over to mix it up.

Amazing ramp and wedge facts

- On a **canal** in Belgium there is a long **ramp** that carries **barges** up a hill in a huge tub of water.
- The ancient Egyptians built earth ramps to carry blocks of stone to the tops of their huge pyramids.
- A ramp makes it easier to move heavy things down as well as up.
- Sports cars and express trains have **wedge**-shaped fronts that **push** the air out of the way as they speed along.
- Airport workers put big wedges called chocks under the wheels of airliners to stop them rolling away by accident.

- Rockets go very, very fast. They have a wedge-shaped nose so they can push easily through the air on the way into space.

Glossary

barge	long, narrow boat that carries different things from place to place
blade	narrow strip of metal with a sharp edge
bow	front end of a ship or boat
canal	channel filled with water that boats travel along
chisel	tool for cutting and shaping wood
device	things that do a job. A clothes peg is a device. So is an electronic calculator.
plough	farm machine that turns over soil in a field to make it ready for new crops to be planted
pneumatic	machine that is worked by air is a pneumatic machine

pull	when you move something closer. To pull towards yourself.
push	when you press on something and move it away. To push away from yourself.
soil	top part of the ground where plants grow. Soil is made from tiny bits of rock and rotting plants.
winch	machine for lifting or pulling heavy objects

More books to read

Ramps and Wedges, Angela Royston (Heinemann Library, 2000)

What do Ramps and Wedges do?, David Glover (Heinemann Library, 1996)

Slopes, Michael Dahl (Franklin Watts, 2001)

Index

C90 2234778

MAJOR DUDES

'No other band managed to let groove and intellect coexist as seamlessly: the most incredible rhythm sections with the most captivating narratives and these crazy chord changes.'

Mark Ronson, 2013

'I don't think I have listened to any band more than Steely Dan. They're a bottomless pit of joy.'

Judd Apatow, 2014